America is Un
RIGHT NOW

"We must notify every American"

Published in the United States by

America in Defilade, Inc.

6 November 2020

Copyright © 2020 **American Fulcrum, Inc.**

Written and Edited by

American Fulcrum, Inc.

ISBN: 978-1-7346086-2-5

Over the many years I have studied military history and the different philosophies of war I have come to 2 irrefutable facts as it relates to the United States of America. First, there are countries right now that are actively working to take over America in order to control our influence on the world and decrease the value of our economy. The generational wealth and global power from this take-over are immeasurable. Second, the United States of America is too strong to defeat militarily so any kind of hostile takeover would need to occur from within our own government.

Make no mistake, plans have been in motion for years by several foreign countries to disable and dismantle the United States of America, but in the last several years the plans have turned into action. America is Under attack "RIGHT NOW". It is happening blatantly out in the open and right in front of us all. There is No Disguise and No Deception needed as the United States of America is being sold and traded piece by piece and deal by deal from within the shadow cells of our own trusted government.

It seems absolutely impossible that such an action could occur in a country as strong as America and with the incredible level of detail that is given to our country's security. But it is in the shadows where decay begins.

It is up to the citizens of the United States of America to save our country and all that is good. We must stand together and fight the injustice that is being pushed upon us and keep lit the American Beacon of Truth and Justice for the world to follow.

- Tim Norton

America is Under Attack RIGHT NOW

Where it Began…

On 11 September 2001 a foreign invader attacked the United States of America. It had been nearly 60 years since a foreign country attacked the United States on American soil. This attack did more than provoke the United States into a nearly 20-year war, it also showed the US government agencies charged with protecting American soil just how vulnerable we were as a country.

In addition to America's vulnerability for attack was the sudden reality that our elected leaders were ineffective at working together. Under the George W. Bush administration there was a constant barrage from the Democratic Party to disqualify his ability to run an effective Presidency. To this end, the US government agencies charged with protecting the United States of America from foreign and domestic enemies (CIA, NSA, FBI) began the process of setting up a "Shadow Government" to ensure the country was safe regardless of what President was in office. At this time (2001) the Department of Homeland Security had not yet been created (25 November 2002) and the Department of Defense was more of a tool for security than a strategic operations group so neither group was a player in operating a "Shadow Government".

The process of setting up a "Shadow Government" was not the primary mission for any of our national security agencies at first. They simply separated themselves into "Cells" - individual organizations that kept and utilized all learned information only for the teams and groups within their organization. By separating into Cells, each agency could work quicker and without direct government oversight. As the United States had been attacked and was now at war with the Middle East, it was easy for each agency to separate themselves into Cells, create and carry out their own operations and in effect become their own branch of government. And as all of this was viewed as being for the greater good of protecting America, it was completely funded and approved by the 3 branches of our then current US government. A major downside of this action (besides being a completely non-elected or governed part of our US government) was the fact that none of the Cells worked together or shared information. Although incredible information was being learned by each separate Cell, none of the information was shared. This would lead to the death of many US service members and be the primary reason for the ineffectiveness of many combat missions.

Fast forward to 20 January 2009, Barack Obama was sworn in as the 44th United States President. Upon swearing his oath to the United States of America, President Obama was given a briefing by each US government agency detailing America's current state of affairs. This would be the first time that the US President was introduced to the "True" situation (OPTEMPO) of the United States as it relates to every foreign and domestic controversy, conflict and threat. Although our national security agencies had been operating independently for the last 8+ years, it was not until President Obama took office that these agencies started to play a major role in running our countries day to day operations (Shadow Government operations begin).

A US Shadow Government is in Place and Begins to Run our Country…

As an incoming President to a country that has been at war since 2001, there was no way for Barack Obama to truly comprehend the complex programs and operations that each agency had implemented in working to keep America safe from foreign threats. And the amount of time and manpower it would take to brief the President and/or any member of his cabinet on the then "current operations" of each agency would have been a monumental task. Furthermore, when Barack Obama was elected as the 44th President of the United States of America his Presidency became more of a celebration of "Accomplishment" and less of a leader to the country. President Obama and his cabinet were never entrusted to the inner workings and operations each agency was performing on behalf of the United States. As each agency saw it, the President and his cabinet were only in office for a maximum of 8 years then a new President would be elected into office. At most this gave any sitting President 8 years of knowledge about the operations and security of the country. Most US government employees within each agency were there for life and while serving in senior leadership positions had 25 and 30 years of experience managing and monitoring the safety of America. So for ease of operation, the Obama administration allowed each agency to continue operating independently thus allowing each agency to gain greater power. Each agency then used this gained power to eventually take over running the domestic and foreign policy of our US government from behind closed doors - "The Shadows".

US Elected Officials Position Themselves for Power and Wealth…

As each of our US Federal Security Agencies were now entrusted with the daily mission of security as well as operations command and control, it allowed more time for the US elected officials of our country to gain their own personal power and wealth. To that end, US elected officials began creating their own "Cells" disguised as legitimate US businesses and Non-Profit Organizations (NPO). These Cells are made up not only of US elected officials but also senior executives of US and Foreign corporations.   The main goal of these Cells is to gain power and wealth through the utilization of US Tax Dollars in the form of US government contracts. As the Obama Presidency and the war continued, more and more US elected officials began creating their own Cells. And US government contracts sponsored by senior US elected officials being issued during a time of war were not often questioned. Soon our US government was as segmented as our US Federal Security Agencies. It did not take long for foreign countries to see the segmentation of our US government and the greed for power and wealth these individual and newly formed Cells were working to attain. This was when the United States of America started to be sold to foreign countries.

Although there were many deals and alliances created with foreign companies and foreign governments by these rouge Cells during the Obama Administration, the biggest were:

1. Clintons (Russia) - Russia paid millions to a U.S. lobbying firm (owned by the Clintons) in an effort to influence then-Secretary of State Hillary Clinton to make sure the deal with Uranium One was successful. You can read more about this action at https://docs.house.gov/meetings/II/II06/20190625/109694/HHRG-116-II06-20190625-SD004.pdf.

2. Obama Faction (Iran) - $1.7 Billion Dollars ($400 million in Euros and other currencies followed by $1.3 billion dollars in cash) delivered to Tehran in a US Jumbo Jet. You can read details about this action at https://www.washingtonpost.com/news/fact-checker/wp/2018/03/01/was-obamas-1-7-billion-cash-deal-with-iran-prohibited-by-u-s-law/.

3. Joe Biden and Hunter Biden (Ukraine) - Joe Biden fosters a deal with the natural gas company Burisma which operates in the Crimea peninsula of Ukraine in which his son Hunter is given a senior executive position with Burisma in exchange for direct access to

the Obama administration. You can read details about this action at https://nypost.com/2020/10/14/email-reveals-how-hunter-biden-introduced-ukrainian-biz-man-to-dad/.

4. Joe Biden and Hunter Biden (China) - Hunter Biden indicates that he accepts an opportunity working for a Chinese billionaire where he is paid an annual fee of $10 million for introductions and another opportunity working for the largest Chinese energy company where he is paid the same. You can read details about this action at https://www.bbc.com/news/world-54553132.

As the alliance between these Cells and their new foreign government partners grew, so did their greed. Soon it was evident that more attention was being given by our US elected officials to their side deals then to running the United States of America.

Donald Trump enters the world of politics…

As a global business icon, Donald Trump has business dealings all over the world. Through his more than 40 years working in foreign nations with senior advisors and officials, Trump has witnessed first-hand the many poor deals our US elected officials have put in place with foreign countries and global organizations. As it has been described, the United States of America has been treated for many years as an open checkbook, handing out money with little to no return on our investment. US Tax Dollars wasted that should have been used to take care of American families and American infrastructure. As Trump has said on numerous occasions, the amount of wasted US dollars and the terrible deals with foreign nations was an embarrassment. Through years of neglect by past Presidential administrations, the United States had become a joke to senior officials and elected leaders of foreign countries. It was time for a change.

On 16 June 2015, Donald Trump formally announced his Presidential candidacy with a campaign rally and speech at Trump Tower in New York City. In his speech, Trump drew attention to domestic issues such as illegal immigration, offshoring of American jobs, the U.S. national debt, and Islamic terrorism. Trump gained immediate acceptance by the American people as he was acknowledging the issues a majority of Americans felt were being neglected by current US elected officials. Trump became the voice of the American people. But what really made Trump dangerous to the Democratic agenda was his independent power and wealth. Trump had no want or need for any further power or wealth and was therefore not able to be influenced by US corporations or foreign relations. It was for this reason that Trump was able to speak his mind on any issue facing America without fear of offending potential future business partners or foreign dignitaries. This immediately resonated positively with a majority of the American people. And that was dangerous to the "New" Democratic Party that had become divided Cells working only for power and wealth.

How the Democratic Party was Maintaining Control of our Government…

The Democratic Party has long held an extremely close, almost incestual relationship with a great many members of the American press - not all of them but most. It has been suggested for years that the people who work in the press are made up of the social outcasts from high schools and colleges from around the world. And as they were never included in social cliques they have a constant need to make the world a more equal and non-judgmental place where everyone is the same regardless of talent, abilities or intelligence. As the Democratic Party's business model has evolved over the years to gaining power (and votes) through the distribution of US Tax Dollars to those they would keep in poverty, they have made a home for the socially awkward members of the press. So a partnership was formed. The Democratic Party pretends to care about less fortunate Americans and the American press sells their lie.

With the power of information comes the power to control thought and emotion of the masses. This has been the primary tool of power for the Democratic Party for years. Utilizing their monopoly of the American press, the Democratic Party has been able to control all aspect of US politics and keep US elected officials in line regardless of their party affiliation. Should a US elected official begin doing something deemed negative by the Democratic Party, key members of the Democratic Party would organize a "Smear Campaign" against that individual and soon their political career would be in jeopardy. This action is less effective against a group but still powerful. As the Democrats honed this craft during the Obama administration into an extremely effective weapon it became almost impossible for any US elected officials with ideas for positive change in America to be heard without the consent of the Democratic Party. This greatly reduced the effectiveness of the Republican Party elected officials and essentially silenced every American voice that did not agree with the Democratic agenda.

With the control of information and the ability to "smear" any individual or corporation that opposed them, the Democratic Party was convinced they were invincible and that the United States of America was theirs to control and own. This arrogance would become the Democratic Party's weakness and was the primary reason for many of their party's members being exposed as frauds to the American people. The exposure of fraudulent and criminal activities would also cost the Democratic Party the 2016 Presidential Election; an election they were certain they could not lose with pollsters and the media touting double digit percentage wins in almost every US state for the Democratic Party.

The 2016 Presidential election was an election the Democrats could not afford to lose as they had just spent the majority of the last 8 years creating alliances with other countries and partnering with foreign corporations for power and wealth. If the details of these illicit alliances were learned by the American people it would cripple the Democratic Party for years to come. The Democrats would have to act quickly to remove Trump from office before Trump or anyone in his administration discovered their "True" allegiance to foreign interests over their allegiance to the United States of America.

The Democrats Launch the "Russian Collusion" Scandal…

When Donald Trump was sworn in as the 45th President of United States on 20 January 2017, American politics were changed forever and the restoration of the United States of America was made a priority. Trump had promised the American people that he was going to "Drain the Swamp" of corrupt politicians (Democrat and Republican) and bring a voice back to all American people. But the idea of an elected official that kept their word to the American people and was not influenced by power or money frightened many politicians - Republican and Democrat. It was primarily for this reason that so many politicians were willing to accept the accusations that Russia was responsible for helping Trump get elected as the President.

In an effort to discredit the legitimacy of Trump's Presidency, the Democratic Party accused Trump and his campaign of working with Russia to help him win the Presidential election. As the US Federal Security Agencies did not want to lose their new found power of running the country from the shadows, they immediately began working with the Democratic Party to create false evidence and bolster lies about Trump. This would become known as the "Russian Collusion Scandal". Essentially the Democratic Party was using their primary weapon of the American press to create false information that would discredit Trump with the American people. The US Federal Security Agencies would then legitimize the false information so the American people would accept it as true.

But their efforts backfired as the American people who had not been heard for so many years refused to listen to the Democratic Party or the American Press. Instead, they held allegiance to President Trump and allowed members of the American press that were loyal to America and the Trump Presidency to search out the truth.   After 2 years and more than $100 million dollars the truth was revealed - there was never any Russian collusion by the Trump campaign.

More importantly, what was revealed to the American people was:

1. America was being run by US Federal Security Agencies during the Obama administration and not a Presidential administration

2. The American press was corrupt and dishonest ("Fake News") with an extreme loyalty to the Democratic agenda

3. The Democratic Party had become a Socialist organization with extreme loyalties to themselves and not the American people.

For the first time in US history the American people were able to see our US elected leaders (Democrats and Republicans) for who they really were, for what they truly believed in and for their corruptness.

It was at the conclusion of the "Russian Collusion Scandal" that American politics became the primary focus of the American people. Never in the history of America were so many Americans involved in politics with a relentless drive for the restoration of American greatness.   And President Trump was the voice of the change in America. The more President Trump kept his word with the American people, the stronger he became as a leader. This was made abundantly clear when multiple scandals were launched by the Democratic Party in 2017 and 2018 involving everything from tax fraud to sexual misconduct allegations but President Trump's poll ratings remained strong. Even a 16 January 2020 impeachment could not separate the American people from President Trump. With this type of loyalty there was no doubt that President Trump would be re-elected in 2020.

The Democratic Party launches the Nuclear Option…

With the pressure of foreign interests on the Democratic Party, it was vital the Democrats use any and all options to win back power in the United States. In less than 4 years the Trump administration had put programs in place that bolstered that American economy while financially crippling countries that did not follow through on their promises to America. In addition, the American people were gaining pride in themselves, working in US businesses and removing themselves from US government dependency. Something had to be done to remove Americans from the workplace, foster fear and uncertainty in the US economy and allow for control of the upcoming US Presidential election. The Coronavirus (COVID-19) provided a solution to all of the issues facing the Democratic Party.

The Coronavirus (COVID-19) was first identified in Wuhan, China in 2019. Although most people who are infected with COVID-19 have mild symptoms, COVID-19 can also cause severe illness and even death. Some groups, including older adults and people who have certain underlying medical conditions, are at increased risk of severe illness. Wuhan, China is the capital of the Hubei Province and is the home to 42 Pharmaceutical contract manufacturing facilities, the majority of which are involved in small molecule API (active pharmaceutical ingredients) manufacturing. The primary function of these pharmaceutical manufacturing facilities is to create, discover, synthesize and develop pharmaceuticals. In addition to being a pharmaceutical and chemical development epicenter, Wuhan is the home to the region's biggest airport and deep-water seaport. Wuhan is often called the Chicago of China and is extremely popular among tourists. If a virus was ever going to be developed and released into the general population, Wuhan is just about the best place for a "Ground Zero".   And if a planned virus distribution was ever going to be successfully executed, releasing it in China just before the Chinese Lunar New Year when hundreds of millions of people will be traveling in an out of China would be just about the best time.

What Benefits Would China Gain By Developing a Deadly Virus Aimed at Their Own Country?

China currently has more than 1.4 billion citizens. The cost and effort to feed, house and care for this many people is astronomical. If a virus could be developed that would quickly spread through a population but only kill the elderly and sick it would reduce the cost of caring for these citizens. As the elderly and sick are not able to work in the communist machine, they are a drain on the common good - easily expendable by the Chinese.

America is Under Attack RIGHT NOW

Why Would China Release a Deadly Virus on Their Own People in November 2019?

In June 2019 citizens in Hong Kong took to the streets in peaceful protests focused on keeping their civil liberties in place from the Chinese government. When Hong Kong was given to China from England in 1997, Hong Kong was promised certain freedoms would remain in place that citizens in mainland China did not have. The Chinese government promised Hong Kong their freedoms would remain in place until at least the year 2047. In the months leading up to June 2019, China worked to pass reform that would remove the promised freedoms from the citizens of Hong Kong and put them more in line with mainland China rule of law. This led to the Hong Kong protests of June 2019. In the following weeks the small protests grew into a massive movement with hundreds of thousands of Hong Kong citizens demanding their freedoms remain. The protests garnered support from people and governments around the world. In the months following June 2019 the protests began growing violent as protestors began clashing with police. Fueled by anger toward the police, as well as the slow erosion of Hong Kong civil liberties, the largely leaderless protests morphed into a broader, more complicated movement focused on protecting freedoms, democracy and Hong Kong's autonomy. The protests grew out of control in October 2019 when an unarmed Hong Kong protestor was shot in the chest by police. In response, the protestors began destroying property and hindering business. The Chinese government viewed the protests as a challenge to their fervent nationalism and was extremely angry to be on the world's stage. Escalating matters, all of this was happening during a heated trade war between China and the United States. China was stuck in a political mess they wanted no part of, but how could they disburse hundreds of thousands of Hong Kong citizens without using force.

Coronavirus was the answer. With the release of Coronavirus into the general Chinese population in November 2019, the panic and fear of millions of Chinese citizens caused them to self-quarantine, removing them from the streets and immediately putting an end to the destruction of property and clashes with the police - all without firing a single bullet.

But in their haste to stop the protests and gain order in their own country, China lost control of the virus containment area and the virus spread uncontrollably. With the 2020 Chinese Lunar New Year fast approaching, Chinese citizens had already begun traveling the world in November and December 2019 taking with them the Coronavirus. It was only a matter of time before the extremely contagious disease became a pandemic.

The Democratic Party Capitalizes on the Pandemic…

It is believed that the United States of America first learned about the Coronavirus in December 2019. Not much was known about the virus in December 2019 but what little was learned in a short time led to President Trump stopping all travel into the US from China. President Trump's CDC (Center for Disease Control) team's initial approach was to try and slow the Coronavirus from reaching our shores. But as we learned just how contagious the virus was, we affirmed that it was only a matter of time before every American would be touched by the virus. Initial quarantine efforts in America saw the stoppage of work and the closing of businesses throughout the United States. The quarantine was meant to slow the spread of the Coronavirus so hospitals and care centers would not be overrun until our American scientist could learn more about the disease. It became a problem of strategy in determining how to save as many American lives as possible while keeping the country moving and working until we could develop a vaccine and eventually, hopefully a cure.

On 15 May 2020, the Trump Administration announced the appointment of Moncef Slaoui as chief advisor and General Gustave F. Perna as chief operating officer of "Operation Warp Speed" (OWS), the administration's national program to accelerate the development, manufacturing, and distribution of COVID-19 vaccines, therapeutics, and diagnostics (medical countermeasures). President Trump's vision for "Operation Warp Speed" was to ensure a vaccine would be available by January 2021. If successful, this would be one of the greatest scientific and humanitarian accomplishments in history. Since January 2020, America's scientists and innovators had been working day and night on this national effort. President Trump refused to accept business-as-usual timelines for vaccines and other essential tools, and instead insisted that America, and the world, needed answers faster.

The continuous "push for results" by President Trump led to a great deal being learned about the Coronavirus in a relatively short period of time. Of great importance was how to treat patients who had contracted the virus, both initially and long term. This learned information is the primary reason that our hospitals and healthcare clinics are able to treat and release patients rather than admit them to our hospitals. According to the CDC (Center for Disease Control) Inpatient Beds Occupied (COVID-19 Patients) data from July 2020 less than 8% of beds were occupied nationally. This data proves that the COVID-19 virus was nowhere near as deadly or physically debilitating to the American people as the American press and the Democratic Party were telling us. Utilizing this type of data as well as other metrics from the CDC and leading medical organizations the Trump administration began the campaign of trying to get America back to work. The continual shutdown of the country was causing detrimental effects that were destroying the social and economic fabric of America. It was vital to our future as Americans that we get back to work and back to each other.

The call for American businesses and American workers to go back to work was a major detriment to the Democratic Party's plan for the 2020 Presidency. If the American people went back to work and realized there were no ill effects from the Coronavirus then the American people would determine the Democratic Party was lying to America (again) and only trying to garner power for their Party. For this reason, the Democratic Party and the American press changed their format in July 2020 of reporting Coronavirus deaths to reporting the number of Coronavirus cases. Obviously as we Americans began to work and socialize together the extremely contagious Coronavirus would be contracted by more Americans. By reporting the number of Coronavirus cases instead of the number of Coronavirus deaths the Democratic Party could continue to instill fear in the American people until the 2020 Presidential election. As long as the Democratic Party and American press pushed the narrative of "Irresponsible Actions" by President Trump in Ignoring the Coronavirus, they believed they had a chance at taking the 2020 Presidential election. The Coronavirus was the only platform that the Democratic Party could run on as (regardless of the Coronavirus pandemic) the American economy was beginning to grow at a record rate, American unemployment was decreasing at a record rate, the number of Coronavirus deaths were less than .01% and a new vaccine was already in the human trials phase with preparation for distribution.

To secure the 2020 Presidential election the plan of the Democratic Party and the American press was to use the Coronavirus to change the rules of voting in the 2020 Presidential election. The first step was to constantly push the number of Coronavirus cases on the American people. Some news channels even showed the number of new Coronavirus cases at the bottom of their television screen like a stock ticker. This would subliminally advertise to anyone who watched those news channels that Americans need to be afraid because the Coronavirus was out to get us all. The second step was to market Coronavirus utilizing face masks. The Democratic Party, the Democratic State Governors and the American press pushed excessively the message of "masking for the Cure" which meant America to put masks on everyone and everything. While the debate still continues on whether wearing a mask even helps in the prevention or contraction of the Coronavirus, it was vital to the Democratic agenda that Americans be forced to see and/or wear a mask as a daily (hourly) subliminal reminder to all Americans of the Coronavirus. It was a Democratic Party marketing tool as much as a safety measure.

The Democratic Party Launches Their Plan to Secure the 2020 Election…

With the hourly bombardment by the Democratic Party and the American press of new Coronavirus cases and the "now more than ever" need for social distancing marketing message, a demand was being made by the Democratic Party for US States to allow for a better social distancing "Voting Process". The formulation of this plan can be seen as early as April 2020 in an article by "The Atlantic". You can read the article here https://www.theatlantic.com/politics/archive/2020/04/voting-mail-2020-race-between-biden-and-trump/609799/.

Once the case for Social Distancing Reform for the American voter was made by the Democratic Party and the American press, the next step was to petition US State legislators in the Presidential election "Swing States" to create the "Voting Process Reform".

A "Swing State" (or battleground state) refers to any state that could reasonably be won by either the Democratic or Republican Presidential candidate by a swing in votes. These states are usually targeted by both major-party campaigns, especially in competitive elections. The US States that regularly lean to a single party are called "Safe States" and generally have a base of support from which they can draw a sufficient share of the electorate without significant investment or effort by their campaign. There were 12 US States identified as "Swing States" for the 2020 Presidential election. They are North Carolina, Florida, Wisconsin, Iowa, Arizona, Pennsylvania, Michigan, Nevada, Georgia, Ohio, New Hampshire and Texas.

Upon confirming the 2020 Presidential election "Swing States", the next primary objective of the Democratic Party was to ensure "Mail in Ballots" would be made available to not just every US Citizen but to every person living in a US "Swing State". To ensure this "Voting Process Reform" happened, the Democratic Party sent over 600 lawyers and more than 10,000 volunteers to these "Swing States" to petition state legislators for "Voting Process Reform".   Almost every US State has state laws that stipulate no election process may be amended or changed unless approved by that states congress and confirmed by that states Supreme Court. Utilizing over 600 lawyers, a campaign was launched by the Democratic Party to use the effects of the Coronavirus on the American population as a reason for "State Emergency Protocols" to be enacted that would allow for "Voting Process Reform".   This reform would be made without consent from each US State's legislators or their US State judiciary office.

16

Details of this plan were in an article published by "Reuters" on 1 July 2020. You can read the article here https://www.reuters.com/article/us-usa-election-biden/biden-pulls-together-hundreds-of-lawyers-as-a-bulwark- against-election-trickery-idUSKBN24305H.

As "Voting Process Reform" became more acceptable to several of the "Swing States", the next push by the Democratic Party was to have "mail in ballots" sent directly to every home in each US State regardless of US citizenship, state identification, criminal status or even confirmation of life. If a US State did not accept that option from the Democratic lawyers, the next alternative being pushed by the Democratic Party was to let every person in that US State be allowed to join a mailing list so they could be sent a "mail in ballot". Again, no proof of anything was required to be added to the mailing list or to be sent a "mail in ballot". The overall objective of the Democratic Party in this phase was to have as many ballots sent to as many people (not just US citizens) as possible in every "Swing State". The Democratic Party would then utilize their more than 10,000 volunteers to go "door to door" and assist people in filling out, signing (or not signing as some "Swing States" did not even require a signature on their mail in ballots) and submitting the "mail in ballots". Multiple "Not For Profit" and "For Profit" organizations joined the effort to assist the Democratic Party ensure as many mail in ballots as possible were filled out, signed and collected. Companies actually recruited and hired people to go "door to door" to assist in filling out and submitting the mail-in ballots. These people were given the name of "Ballot Mules".

Working to subvert and quell any objections from logical and "Free-Thinking" Americans in the United States, the Democratic Party launched a huge campaign with the American press to tell Americans just how difficult it would be to defraud the "mail in ballot" election process. The American press wanted Americans to know just silly they were to think that an American Presidential election could be manipulated by mail-in ballots. But Americans were about to witness the greatest Presidential election fraud in US history. Once all the mail in ballots were collected, they were held at their respective polling stations until the night of the 2020 Presidential election. By holding these ballots, the Democratic Party could monitor the election results as "In Person" voting was reported and then work to calculate how many mail in ballots would be needed to secure victory for the Democratic candidate at each polling station. The entire operation almost failed when President Trump received a far greater number of votes than the Democrats had projected - The most Presidential election votes ever received by a sitting US President. It was for this reason that for the first time in modern US election history, multiple polling stations were forced to stop counting votes and shut down. The Democrats were in firm control of each state's polling headquarters utilizing Coronavirus quarantining protocols to keep them locked down. As such, the Democrats were able to keep "Poll Watchers" out of various polling headquarters giving them the time necessary in the overnight hours to issue enough mail in ballots to each swing state's polling station to ensure a Democratic victory.

America is Under Attack RIGHT NOW

The Great Presidential Election Fraud of November 2020 – Step by Step

Tuesday 3 November 2020 marked the final day for Presidential election voting and traditionally is the day for the most "in-person" voting. Most voting polls close at 7:00pm local time with a few states opting for a 7:30pm to 9:00pm close. Voting polls may be authorized additional voting hours by their US state should an unforeseen circumstance arise requiring more time be allotted for voters. But the majority of votes by US voters have been cast by 7:30pm local. At the culmination of voting activities each US state begins their own individual process for counting and reporting the votes.

The information below is a rough timeline of the expected reporting of unofficial results on election night 3 November 2020. These times are approximate and based on past elections. Any significant extension of voting hours at any location in a US state would affect these times. Reporting times will vary by county in each US State.

- 7:00 p.m. - 9:00 p.m. Polls close.

- 7:30 p.m. - 9: 30 p.m. Early votes are reported.

  o One-stop early votes and absentee by-mail votes that have been approved by a county board of elections (CBE) are reported in both the "Media File" and on the "Election Results Dashboard".

  o Data is refreshed approximately every 5~10 minutes.

- 7:30 p.m. - 9:30 p.m. Precinct official's hand-deliver results to CBEs.

- 8:30 p.m. - 1:00 a.m. Precinct results are reported.

  o Results appear in the "Media File" and on the "Election Results Dashboard".

  o Data is refreshed approximately every 5~10 minutes.

- After Election Night

  o Absentee ballots that are postmarked on or before Election Day and received by the county board of elections by the return deadline, as well as provisional votes, will be added to the results as they are approved by CBEs during the canvass period after Election Night.

**

Reporting the Results…

As soon as the first voting polls officially close, news agencies around the country begin to project voting results data by polling exit voters (Americans that are leaving the polls after casting their vote), past voting history of each county in the US State and polling data from pollsters and polling companies that was performed prior to the election. Almost every news agency uses the firm "Edison Research" for exit polls and results as they come in from each precinct (a precinct is the smallest unit into which voting districts are divided - typically counties are subdivided into precincts based on addresses). The voting data is then provided to the American people. Most Americans watch the election results on TV news channels. This year Nielsen measured 56.9 million viewers of the 2020 Presidential election coverage which was down from the 71.4 million viewers who watched the 2016 Presidential election. With 21 different news networks reporting on the Presidential election, the majority of Americans by far watched the election results on the FOX News channel (13.6 million viewers - the most in history).

The FOX News channel utilizes a special Presidential election Studio to present the election results to the American people. Among other reporting tools, their reporting coverage includes news anchors, a voting probability analyst and an election day results map in the shape of the United States which is color coded to correspond with election results. With these tools the Fox News channel brings the Presidential election to life for their viewers.

The First Signs of Election Fraud are seen by millions of Americans "Live"…

The Fox News channel began their 8 hour "Live" Presidential election night coverage at 6:00pm EST with leading anchors Bret Baier and Martha MacCallum accompanied by several co-anchors and contributors who joined them for commentary and analysis. As election results came into the Fox News studio, the color coded map began to fill in as election voter numbers were posted to each US State. At the beginning of election night there were varied results as the number of "Early Election" votes were counted, submitted and added to the color coded map. The initial "Early Election" voting numbers slightly favored the Democratic Party but as the 3 November 2020 election day votes came in, the vote numbers moved in President Trump's favor. The swing was so great that at 9:20pm EST Brit Hume (Fox News co-anchor) announced that the betting companies had revised their betting odds of President Trump being reelected from 39% to 64.8%. Those odds would grow to more than 70% by 11:00pm.

At the same time, China announced that the Yuan (the Chinese currency) had plunged 1.4% against the US dollar based on the current election results. You can read more about the plunge of the Chinese Yuan at https://www.cnn.com/2020/11/04/investing/china- yuan-us-election-intl-hnk/index.html.

With disaster looming for the Democratic Party and China being faced with 4 more years of Tariffs and trade deals that favored the United States, the Presidential election vote results slowed significantly or stopped completely in 9 of the 12 "Swing States". They were North Carolina, Wisconsin, Iowa, Arizona, Pennsylvania, Michigan, Nevada, Georgia and Ohio. It was an incredible phenomenon to watch it "live" on the Fox News channel because no one had ever seen election vote counting stopped by so many US States at the same time. To add to the phenomenon, the US State of Florida which has the 3rd highest population of any US State at 21.6 million residents had completed nearly all of their vote counting (96%) by 11:00pm EST.   This incredible series of actions led to many unanswered questions that need to be answered by our government:

1. Why did so many of the "Swing States" (much smaller than Florida) seem to stop counting votes and fail to report their vote count numbers on election night 2020?
2. Was the votes counting stopped to allow for "fraudulent mail in votes" to be requested and added to each of the 9 controversial "Swing States" voting totals?
3. Why were "Poll Watchers" kept out of certain polling stations in the overnight hours of election night 2020?
4. Without the presence of the "Poll Watchers" who had oversight and confirmation of the mail in ballot counting process?

The Post Election Day votes Do Not Follow the Same Voting Pattern as Every Other Presidential Election in US History…

Below are the Presidential election totals as reported by the Fox News channel for the 9 "Swing States" that stopped reporting votes at 11:00pm EST - the point where vote counting seemed to stop for most of the "Swing States".   These vote totals include early voting and a great majority of the 3 November 2020 election day votes. The "mail in ballot" votes have not yet been added to these vote totals.

Swing State	Votes for Trump	Percent of Votes	Votes for Biden	Percent of Votes	Percent of Votes In
North Carolina	2,730,890	50.1%	2,655,149	48.7%	94%
Wisconsin	1,438,989	51.2%	1,330,889	47.3%	88%
Michigan	1,866,604	53.6%	1,557,530	44.7%	64%
Ohio	2,993,270	53.5%	2,526,931	45.1%	94%
Iowa	896,100	53.2%	757,707	45.0%	98%
Nevada	496,166	48.1%	536,759	51.9%	66%
Arizona	1,114,185	45.5%	1,304,461	53.2%	74%
Pennsylvania	2,703,112	56.7%	2,009,967	42.1%	64%
Georgia	2,366,242	51.3%	2,248,032	48.7%	93%

From these results we can see that President Trump had a large lead over Biden in almost every "Swing State".   With a majority of the votes having been counted in these 9 "Swing States" you can see the voting pattern that has occurred from the early voting and 3 November 2020 votes as an average of 80% of the votes had been counted. The only way this pattern would change is through the manipulation of votes that have not been counted - "mail in ballots".   The odds of the "Swing State" voter "mail in ballots" to be different from the voting pattern developed from all the other votes collected by every other citizen in their respective US State would be astronomical. But that is exactly what the Democratic Party and the American press want the American people to believe. They want us to accept that the last small percentage of "Swing State" voters who voted by "mail in ballot" nearly all voted for Biden – the Democratic Candidate.

America is Under Attack RIGHT NOW

Democrats and the American Press Want America to Believe the Staggering Number of American Votes Cast in the 2020 Presidential Election is a Normal Voting Turnout…

Utilizing all of the modern voting election records (which started with the 1932 election and continue through the 2016 election) we can determine that the average percentage of American voters that vote in any US Presidential election is 55.8%. That means that in the last 22 elections the average voter turnout has been about 55.8% of the US population registered to vote. For the 2020 Presidential election the voter election totals are nearly 72%. Accounting for Americans that do not vote as a matter of choice as well as Americans that are not able to vote (disabled, incarcerated, medical, etc.) it would be nearly impossible to have 72% of the American voting population vote in the 2020 Presidential election. Even the 2016 Presidential election (Trump - Clinton) which included the first ever female Presidential candidate in American history only garnered votes from 59.2% of the American voting population. And the 2016 Presidential election was much more influential with the American people as 20 million more Americans followed the 2016 Presidential election day coverage than followed the 2020 Presidential election day coverage as confirmed by the Neilson ratings which tracked every viewer of both US Presidential election day coverages.

So, the Democratic Party and the American Press are asking Americans to believe that millions of registered US voters that have never voted in any other election showed up during the Coronavirus pandemic to vote in an election that garnered interest from 20 million fewer Americans. And so many Americans showed up to vote in the 2020 Presidential election that a record 72% of the American voting population voted. Neither the math nor the voting history of every other Presidential election in US history from 1932 till present day can support this claim.

Furthermore, as the next chart details, the number of votes cast in the 9 "Swing States" exceeds the total number of votes cast in the 2016 election by an incredibly large percentage.

Some as high as a 25% difference from the 2016 Presidential election and more than 30% higher than the average percentage of votes in all the other US Presidential elections combined since 1932. Again, it is extremely unlikely that the millions and millions of American voters from these 9 "Swing States" were convinced to vote in this Presidential election. The much more likely scenario was fraudulent "mail in ballots" were cast in lieu of American voter participation. The math does not support any claim that the Democratic Party or the American press is pushing about American voter turnout.

Swing State	2020 Votes for Trump	2020 Votes for Biden	2020 Total Votes	2016 Votes for Trump	2016 Votes for Clinton	2016 Total Votes	2016 to 2020 Vote Total Difference	2016 to 2017 Percent Difference
North Carolina	2,733,645	2,658,274	5,391,919	2,362,631	2,189,316	4,551,947	839,972	15.6%
Wisconsin	1,610,030	1,630,570	3,240,600	1,405,284	1,382,536	2,787,820	452,780	14.0%
Michigan	2,644,525	2,790,648	5,435,173	2,279,543	2,268,839	4,548,382	886,791	16.3%
Ohio	3,074,418	2,603,731	5,678,149	2,841,005	2,394,164	5,235,169	442,980	7.8%
Iowa	896,100	757,707	1,653,807	800,983	653,669	1,454,652	199,155	12.0%
Nevada	625,784	657,248	1,283,032	512,058	539,260	1,051,318	231,714	18.1%
Arizona	1,612,733	1,631,286	3,244,019	1,252,401	1,161,167	2,413,568	830,451	25.6%
Pennsylvania	3,314,164	3,355,387	6,669,551	2,970,733	2,926,441	5,897,174	772,377	11.6%
Georgia	2,455,305	2,465,500	4,920,805	2,089,104	1,877,963	3,967,067	953,738	19.4%

Were Pre-Election Polling Numbers Skewed "High" to Reduce Suspicion of Voting Fraud...

The polling numbers from the 2016 Presidential election were a disaster for the Democratic Party. The pre-election polling numbers touted a double digit Presidential win for Hilary Clinton and remained at that level all the way up to election day. This blunder by the Democratic Party and the American press was an embarrassment and showed they had no connection with the American people. There is no way the Democratic Party or the American press would make the same mistake twice. So, it was very suspect when the American people were told by the American press that Biden had double digit "Swing State" leads in 2020 pre-election Presidential polling. But it makes perfect sense if the Democratic Party and the American press were planning to "Take" the election by using "mail in ballots". Having hundreds of thousands of mail in ballots at their disposal they could set the margin of victory to almost any level and gain back the message that the Democratic Party was in touch with the American people.

There was a problem however as there was no way for the Democratic Party to know just how many mail-in ballots they would need to win in the 12 "Swing States". While they had tens of thousands of paid contractors and volunteers working in the "Swing States" collecting ballots, there was no way to determine the exact number of ballots that would be needed to win each "Swing State". If too many mail-n ballots were added by the Democrats prior to the election day votes being counted they could greatly surpass their projected pre-election polling numbers and immediately create a case for investigation for election tampering. The only way to add enough mail-in ballots with accuracy would be to first see how many votes would be needed to win the election and then submit that amount on election night.

The Democratic Party knew that Trump's popularity had gown greatly among the American people during his Presidency and for that reason they would need to collect a massive amount of mail-in ballots. To keep the American people from suspicion of foul play after the election, the Democratic Party and the American press would use the high "Biden Win" pre-election polling numbers to coax the American people into believing that Biden was the choice of the American people for the next Presidency. But while the American voters were watching to see which candidate had the most votes, they never looked at the total amount of votes that were actually being counted.

What the Democratic Party and the American press did not count on were the millions of American voters that were going to vote for President Trump, especially in the "Swing States" where he was showing landslide victory voting numbers the night of the 2020 election. The table below shows the number of votes cast for Trump's 2020 election in the 9 controversial "Swing States" actually increased by hundreds of thousands of American votes from the 2016 Presidential election. It was for this reason that by 11:00pm EST a majority of the American people thought Trump was going to be re-elected to the Presidency.

The amount of American votes Trump was receiving was something the Democratic Party did not count on and they started scrambling to correct their error. They began by getting multiple "Swing States" loyal to the Democratic agenda to slow down and even stop the vote counting process. This action would provide enough time to determine the number of "mail in ballots" needed to push Biden past Trump in the 2020 election. In some of the "Swing States" nearly 800,000 votes were needed just too equal Trumps vote count. And that is exactly what happened. For the first time in modern US Presidential Election history, nearly all of the controversial "Swing States" suspended vote counting the night of the Presidential Election, allowed mail-in ballots to be added, then resumed vote counting the following day. And the American people are to believe that of the more than 800,000 mail in ballots added, nearly every vote was for Biden. Yet another absolute impossibility that the Democratic Party and the American press are asking the American people to believe.

Swing State	2020 Votes for Trump	2016 Votes for Trump	2016 to 2020 Vote Total Difference	2016 to 2020 Vote Precent Difference
North Carolina	2,733,645	2,362,631	371,014	13.6%
Wisconsin	1,610,030	1,405,284	204,746	12.7%
Michigan	2,644,525	2,279,543	364,982	13.8%
Ohio	3,074,418	2,841,005	233,413	7.6%
Iowa	896,100	800,983	95,117	10.6%
Nevada	625,784	512,058	113,726	18.2%
Arizona	1,612,733	1,252,401	360,332	22.3%
Pennsylvania	3,314,164	2,970,733	343,431	10.4%
Georgia	2,455,305	2,089,104	366,201	14.9%

America is Under Attack RIGHT NOW

Time To "Wake Up" America...

So now America and the American people are at a crossroad.   First, we must all shoulder some of the blame as we the American people have allowed the Democrats Party and the American press to sneak this election by us.   Every American voter should have been "Awaken" to the absolute power the Democratic Party yields within the American Press by the Hunter Biden scandal and the lack of coverage it garnered from the American Press.   A textbook "cover-up" and a slap in the face to the American people.   It would do well for all Americans to remember that we give power to the press - not the other way around.   Next, the American people must insist on fair, equal, open, honest elections for ALL American elections.   One man, One woman, One vote.   Register to vote as a legal US Citizen and cast your One vote.   That's it.

The Alarm was Sounded But Did You Hear It America...

On 14 October 2020 the New York Post reported that Joe Biden knew of, and potentially participated in, his son's business dealings in China and Ukraine. The Post published incriminating content from a cache of emails the newspaper obtained from a laptop Hunter Biden reportedly dropped off at a Delaware computer repair shop. The computer repair store owner claimed he found lewd images and video of the former vice President's son on the hard drive, along with emails suggesting Hunter Biden arranged a meeting between Joe Biden and an executive of the Ukrainian gas company Burisma.

Hunter Biden joined Burisma's board in 2014 after his father Joe Biden became the Obama administration's chief liaison for Ukraine, a country that is riddled with political corruption. Joe Biden pushed former Ukrainian President Petro Poroshenko to fire a prosecutor who was reportedly investigating Burisma or lose US Federal aid money. This story was verified by Joe Biden when he was taped telling the story to a group during a Democratic fund raiser.

While the New York Post initially reported the compromised laptop of Hunter Biden, it was the Federalist magazine that obtained text messages on 22 October 2020 allegedly showing Hunter Biden orchestrating a meeting between his father Joe Biden and Hunter's former business partner, Tony Bobulinski. The text message went on to say the meeting was to discuss a proposed business venture with China Energy company (CEFC).

Bobulinski was the former CEO of SinoHawk Holdings, which Hunter claims was a partnership between CEFC Chairman Ye Jianming, Hunter, and Joe Biden's brother, Jim Biden.   In a joint report released by the US Senate Homeland Security and Senate Finance Committees it was made known that Ye Jianming had ties to the People's Liberation Amy.

America is Under Attack RIGHT NOW

Joe Biden Lies about his Involvement with His Son's Business Dealings…

Biden's Presidential campaign has denied that Joe Biden ever benefited from any financial transactions with foreign entities, though Joe Biden has not yet responded to a 22 October 2020 Fox News report suggesting he took part in a meeting with one of Hunter's former business partners. Hunter Biden allegedly consulted with his father Joe Biden about a venture with now-bankrupt Chinese oil company CEFC China Energy. Sinclair Broadcast Group reporter James Rosen confirmed in an October 2020 report that the FBI opened up a criminal investigation into Hunter Biden back in 2019. Rosen conducted an exclusive interview with Hunter Biden's former business partner Tony Bobulinski in which he said if Joe Biden were elected to the Presidency he would definitely be compromised by China.

To add merit to Tony Bobulinski's claim, he produced three phones during a press conference that supposedly contained incriminating information about the CEFC meeting. The Senate Homeland Security and Governmental Affairs Committee and the Senate Finance Committee interviewed Bobulinski the 3rd week of October 2020 to discuss his knowledge of "the Biden family business plans with Chinese, of which [Joe Biden] was plainly familiar at least at a high level". Bobulinksi also made it known clearly in this meeting that Joe Biden was not telling the truth in his claims to have never discussed business with his son Hunter. "That is false," Bobulinski said of Joe Biden's previous statements. "I have firsthand knowledge about this because I directly dealt with the Biden family, including Joe Biden."

The head of one conservative watchdog group believes the emails and laptops are legitimate. Government Accountability Institute President Peter Schweizer told Sinclair Broadcast Group's Kristine Frazao Monday that the emails match up with what he has found scouring through Joe Biden and Hunter Biden's records. "There is no question in my mind those emails appear to be genuine, particularly because some of them dovetail very well with emails that we obtained from other sources," said Schweizer.

The Daily Caller News Foundation obtained an original copy on Wednesday of Hunter Biden's alleged laptop from Giuliani. After receiving the copy, the DCNF provided cyber security firm Errata Security founder Robert Graham with a copy of the email for forensic analysis -- Graham used a cryptographic signature found in the email's metadata to validate that Vadym Pozharsky, an advisor to Burisma's board of directors, emailed Hunter Biden on April 17, 2015, thanking Joe Biden's son for inviting him to Washington, D.C. to speak with his father.

The Media and Tech Companies "Blackout" the New York Posts Hunter Biden Article…

Reporters effectively blacked out the story arguing the New York Post's reporting was part of a Russian disinformation campaign to prop up President Trump. However, the Director of National Intelligence (DNI) John Ratcliff said on 19 October 2020 that there is no evidence to suggest the laptop is part of a Russian disinformation campaign.

The Information "Blackout" by the media was seen on '60 Minutes' with host Lesley Stahl insisting in an interview with the President Trump that the alleged emails and laptop "can't be verified". Also National Public Radio (NPR), which receives US taxpayer money for its operating costs, said in a 22 October 2020 tweet that the allegations were a "waste" of readers' time.

Next the Tech companies worked to provide disinformation to the American people. Facebook and Twitter were even more explicit in working to suppress the distribution of the New York Post's story.

Twitter began blocking tweets from users who were posting the 14 October 2020 New York Post article, telling people that the article violates platform policy because it contained potentially hacked content and private information. Twitter is quoted as saying to their users; "We can't complete this request because this link has been identified by Twitter or our partners as being potentially harmful". In addition, Twitter blocked the New York Post's Twitter account from being able to Tweet the article. There is still no evidence thus far that the New York Post relied on hacked materials for its report.

Facebook spokesman Andy Stone tweeted on 14 October 2020 that the company is "reducing the distribution" of the New York Post's article. He said the move is "part of our standard process to reduce the spread of misinformation". Facebook CEO Mark Zuckerberg and his counterpart at Twitter, Jack Dorsey, testified remotely before the Senate 22 October 2020 to discuss several topics, including the degree to which their platform suppressed mention of the New York Post's report. During this hearing Jack Dorsey told Senator Ted Cruz, R-Texas that Twitter changed its policies after being called to account for their actions. Dorsey said the New York Post can have its account back and repost the article provided the New York Post newspaper deletes the original article.

These bold moves by the media and US Tech companies bring up several glaring questions:

1. Do the Media and Tech Companies really have the guts to fight against the US Senate and purposely control what the American people are allowed to learn and share through their social media apps or did they know in advance the Presidential election results would give power back to the Democrats?

2. Were the media and tech companies in the loop about the fraudulent votes that were going to be used to steal the 2020 Presidential election?

3. And an even more important question - "have these groups been part of the fraudulent vote operation since its inception"

How Does America Fix This...

So here we are as Americans feeling helpless and saddened that our great country has been taken over by a hostile regime. We are fearful for our future as promises of a "Socialist Agenda" have been made by the Democratic Party, the American press and the foreign countries that have worked so hard to put the Democratic Party in power.

Questions most Americans are asking themselves Right Now:

1. How Did the Republicans win so many house seats back and maintain control of the Senate but lose the Presidency?

2. Did the "Fraudulent Ballot Operation" by the Democratic Party also help Governors and other Democratic officials get elected or reelected as a payoff for their help with the operation?

3. Were fraudulent mail-in ballots also used to get Democratic Governors and other Democratic officials elected?

What we can expect next from the Democratic Party:

1. The American press will continue to sell the lie that Biden was the winner of the 2020 Presidential election and that he is capable of running our country.

2. Democrats will now stop reporting on the number of Coronavirus cases in the United States and instead begin reporting the number of diminished Coronavirus deaths.

3. Democrats will claim that they are responsible for the Coronavirus vaccine and bringing that vaccine to the American people when in fact the vaccine is most likely already available and being distributed to all of our US States.

4. As the Coronavirus vaccine is made available to the American people we will all begin to go back to work. As America re-opens it is natural that our economy will grow. You can definitely expect the Democratic Party to take credit for the American economy growing.

Where can we learn how to fix our America:

1. Read the book; *"Building the American Fulcrum"*

What President Trump and the Trump Administration Should Do Next…

It would seem there were a great many dishonest people fighting against the re-election of the Trump administration. The fight to challenge illegal votes may take several weeks if the courts even allow an investigation. While continuing the fight, the Trump administration should push for the following actions:

1. President Trump should sign an "Executive Order" immediately releasing a 2nd Coronavirus Stimulus Package to the American people. As America is moving into the Thanksgiving and Christmas holiday season it would provide an immediate spending boost to the American economy thereby removing a stimulated economy merit for the Democratic Party.

2. If there is a Coronavirus vaccine ready for distribution the Trump administration needs to release it as soon as possible. Not only would the Trump administration be given credit with creating a vaccine for the American people (and the world) in record time, but it would also jump start the American economy prior to President Trump leaving office.

3. If the distribution of the Coronavirus vaccine and the distribution of a 2nd Coronavirus Stimulus Package could happen together just in time for the Christmas shopping season it would most likely create the biggest economic boost to the US economy in the history of America.

4. All of these accomplishments could then be used as campaign points for President Trumps run for the 2024 Presidential election.

What we must do now is to fight. It is vital to our future selves that we not let our country fall into the hands of a socialist regime. We believe that millions of American's have been caught off guard by the Democratic agenda and to just what lengths they will go to in order to destroy America. We may be late to this fight but hopefully the "True Americans" are waking up. We must work together to keep this fraudulent Presidency from destroying our American way of life. Study this paper and start doing some research yourself. We have to get smarter and stronger to stop the Democratic political agenda to steal and sell America.

Notes

Notes

_____

Made in the USA
Columbia, SC
02 October 2024

43484081R00020